NEWPORT HISTORY BYTES
50 Fast Facts

Newport Historical Society

Designed and produced by AFA Publishing

www.afapublishing.com
Antiques & Fine Art Magazine

Copyright © 2014 Newport Historical Society
ISBN: 978-0-9886031-2-7

TABLE OF CONTENTS

    4   Introduction

COLONIAL NEWPORT
- 6   Franklin Press
- 8   River Lane
- 9   John Bradshaw, Regicide
- 10 The Guns of the Colonial Sloop *Tartar*
- 11 Homework in Colonial Newport
- 12 Jewish Burials in Newport
- 13 John Handy and the Colony House
- 14 The Boston Tea Party
- 16 The Newport Post Office
- 18 Orphaned Gravestones
- 20 Slavery and Lotteries
- 22 Memorable Rhode Island Names
- 24 Manumission Documents

19TH CENTURY NEWPORT
- 26 *USS Constitution*
- 28 The National Anthem's Newport Connection
- 30 Jane Stuart
- 32 The *Charles W. Morgan*
- 34 Santa Claus and Newport
- 36 Valentines
- 37 Mrs. George T. Downing
- 38 *Twelve Years a Slave*
- 40 The Final Resting Places of Oliver Hazard Perry
- 42 The Final Resting Places of Commodore Matthew C. Perry
- 44 Fraunces Tavern

46 Edwin Booth of Middletown
48 Newport and President Lincoln
50 Emma Lazarus
52 Anna Harriette Leonowens
54 Roller Skating in Newport
56 Calling Cards
58 Newport Greenhouses
60 Poinsettias and Newport
62 John Singer Sargent in Newport
64 Newport's Royal Wedding

20TH CENTURY NEWPORT

66 Newport's *Titanic* Passengers 1912
68 The Malbones of *Downton Abbey*
70 The Rockefellers
72 Airships in Newport
74 Let's Split: The Levi Gale House
76 Van Johnson
78 King Edward and King George
79 Pearl Harbor and Newport
80 The United Nations and Newport
82 The Kennedy Wedding
86 Presidential Visits
88 *Dark Shadows*
90 Christo and Jeanne-Claude Wrap Newport
92 Cunard Line Visits Newport
94 *Amistad*
96 Queen Elizabeth

All images represented in this book are photographs, objects or documents from the Newport Historical Society's collections, unless otherwise noted.

History 3 *Bytes*

INTRODUCTION

From the city's founding in 1639 to the present day, the history of Newport County overflows with interesting stories. These stories are not just quaint or of local interest; they represent a dynamic history that helps to tell the story of our country. When we established the *History Bytes* blog in 2011, the entries were intended to highlight this rich history in a short, easy to read format. Given the countless stories we have to tell, and that the "bytes" are generally unexpected, amusing, or both, it's not surprising that the blog was an immediate success.

As the posts are shared through social media and local publications, they provide glimpses of interesting moments from the past, many of which have long been forgotten.

If you enjoy reading *Newport History Bytes* we encourage you to follow the latest entries on the Historical Society's website at NewportHistory.org, check out *Gladys,* our online collections database, or "tour" the historic city through our app *Explore Historic Newport* at NewportHistoryApp.com.

Newport's history is American history. It's a resource from which we learn about ourselves and our past, to better inform our future.

Bertram Lippincott III, History Bytes Creator

Elizabeth Sulock, Editor

COLONIAL NEWPORT

FRANKLIN PRESS

Around 1717, James Franklin of Boston, Benjamin Franklin's older brother, began printing on a press he imported from London. By 1727 he had moved to Newport and established a printing and publishing business that would endure for centuries.

Through a succession of family members and partners, *The Newport Mercury* was started in 1758, religious and political pamphlets were distributed and Rhode Island's copy of The Declaration of Independence was made available to all. The old press was retired by 1851 and acquired by the Massachusetts Charitable Mechanics Association and placed on display at the Franklin Institute in Philadelphia. Since 1993 it has been on exhibit at the Museum of Newport History where it can be seen today.

In 2014, Washington Square was awarded the Historic Site in Journalism Award by the Society of Professional Journalists to honor the locations in which the Franklin Press operated.

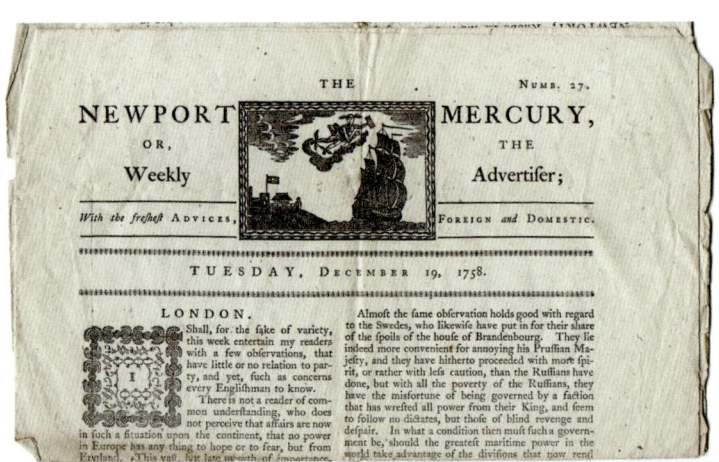

A 1758 issue of *The Newport Mercury* printed on the Franklin Press.

The Franklin Press, on display at the Museum of Newport History.

History 7 Bytes

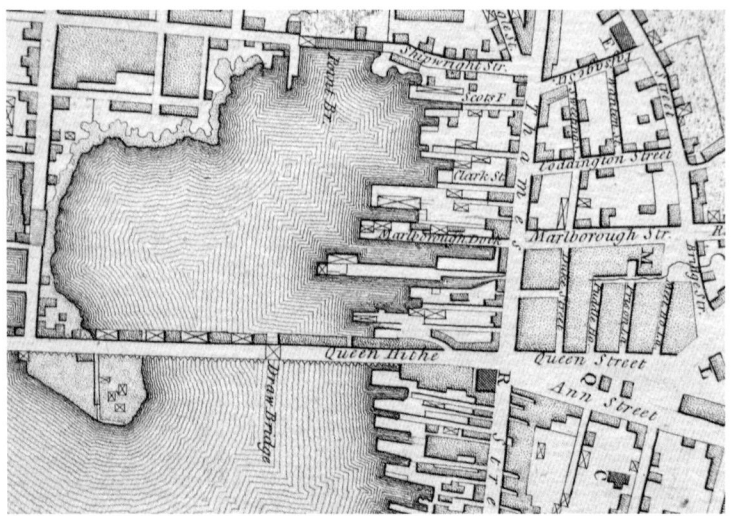

Detail from the 1777 Charles Blaskowitz Map showing River Lane near Marlborough Street.

RIVER LANE

Newport is known for its winding, narrow, and often times random one-way streets. One of these mini streets is River Lane, an alley that runs parallel to Malborough Street.

The site of an ancient river that originated at Clarke's Lane (Oak Street), it ran south on Tanner Street (Marcus Wheatland Boulevard), crossed Marlborough Street and continued west behind the present-day location of Del Nero Cleaners and the Jail House Inn. That river still runs underground, emptying into Newport Harbor at the corner of Long Wharf and Perrotti Park.

Restoration work at Liberty Square, across from the White Horse Tavern, exposed the river flowing in a channel of granite bulkheads. The curved section of the lane at Broadway and Farewell Street was once called Cinnamon Alley.

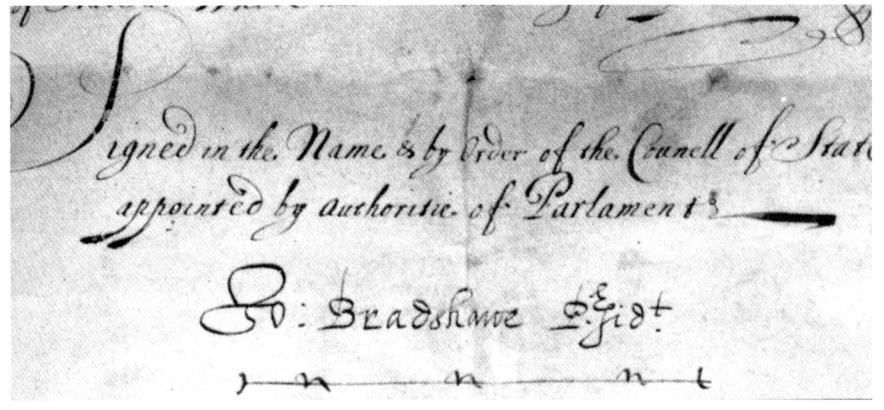

Detail from the Coddington Commission featuring John Bradshaw's signature, issued under Oliver Cromwell's Parliament in 1651.

JOHN BRADSHAW, REGICIDE

In 1649, Rhode Island colonists were busy establishing new communities and Providence was hammering out the last details of its Charter. In Newport, William Coddington was annoyed by governmental and territorial disputes with Providence, the Massachusetts Bay Colony and Plymouth Plantations.

To solve this problem, Coddington made an arrangement with Parliament to proclaim himself Governor of Aquidneck Island for life in 1651. This Coddington Commission, in the collection of the Newport Historical Society, was signed by John Bradshaw, President of the Council of State and affixed with the Great Seal of Oliver Cromwell.

Needless to say, other Rhode Islanders were not amused and sent John Clarke to have the document nullified the following year. Earlier John Bradshaw (1602-1659) had set his hand and seal on another notable document: The Death Warrant of King Charles I at Westminster Hall on 30 January 1649.

Guns from the *Tartar* sit outside the Newport Historical Society's Headquarters.

THE GUNS OF THE COLONIAL SLOOP *TARTAR*

In order to address hostilities during the King George's War, the Rhode Island General Assembly voted to build a sloop in 1740. She was 115 tons, cost £8,679, and was named the *Tartar,* after the *H.M.S. Tartar* which visited from England in 1737. Rhode Island's new Sloop of War had a distinguished and well documented career, particularly at the 1774–1745 Battle of Louisbourg.

The *Tartar* was decommissioned in 1748 and her inventory sold on Goat Island at public auction. The unclaimed items were stored at Fort George for many years. Eventually two of her twelve guns were recovered and used as traffic control posts at the foot of Washington Square.

In 1934 the Newport Historical Society rescued the guns and mounted them on the lawn of the Touro Street headquarters where they can be seen today.

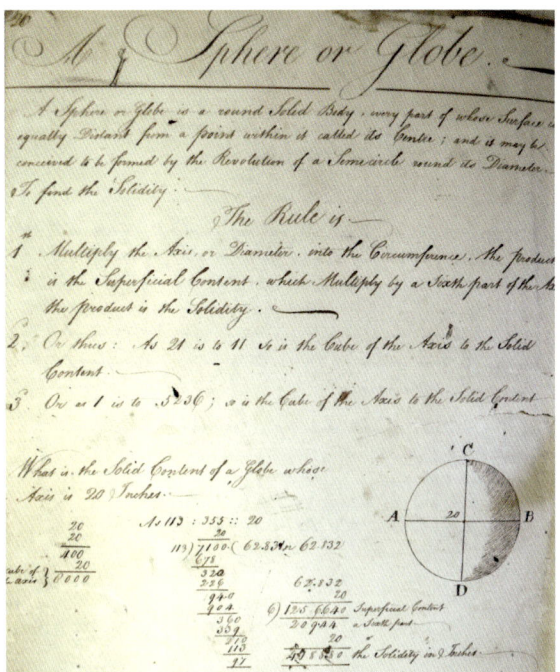

William Engs workbook showing the geometric calculations of a sphere.

HOMEWORK IN COLONIAL NEWPORT

While students today roll their eyes at homework and make excuses to avoid their times tables, the concept of assignments outside the classroom is not new.

Capt. William Engs (1720–1800), who moved from Boston to Newport as a master mariner with experience as a bookkeeper and clerk, was one of Newport's early educators. In 1772 he established a school and took on boarders to study navigation, astronomy, astrology, geography, geometry, double entry accounting and penmanship. The school lasted through the Revolution until 1797 leaving a record of students, subjects and tuition payments (made by parents or wealthy patrons). These records are now part of the Newport Historical Society's collection.

A *Newport Daily News* glass plate negative showing the gates on Farewell Street.

JEWISH BURIALS IN NEWPORT

Though the corner of Bellevue Avenue and Kay Street is a hub of traffic and commerce today, it has been the location of the Jewish cemetery since 1677. The cemetery is in fact much older than Touro Synagogue, located just down the hill, which was built nearly a century later in 1763.

Sephardic Jews established a presence in Newport in 1658. This cemetery contains 38 marked graves dating from 1761–1866, and is enclosed by gates donated in 1842 by Judah Touro. Other early Newport families are buried in lower Manhattan, Philadelphia, New Orleans and the Caribbean.

After a long dormancy in the 19th century, Touro Synagogue experienced a rebirth through a new generation of Ashkenazi worshippers. Under the leadership of Max Levy, Jewish burial lots were purchased in Newport's Braman Cemetery on Farewell Street and fenced off from non-Jewish graves, a required practice of Orthodox Jews. A wrought iron fence with granite and limestone entrance gates graced Farewell Street and the site was formally dedicated on Memorial Day (Decoration Day) 1911.

A 1796 miniature portrait of Major John Handy.

JOHN HANDY AND THE COLONY HOUSE

Each year on Independence Day, Newporters gather on Washington Square to hear the Declaration of Independence read on the Colony House steps, just as citizens did in July 1776 when Major John Handy first "proclaimed" or publicly read aloud the document from that location.

Exactly fifty years after he first read the document, Major John Handy, age 70, ascended the Colony House steps and "forcefully" read the Declaration under a custom built, decorated arch "on that identical spot." Amid the cannon fire and church bells of that celebration, Thomas Jefferson and John Adams had both passed away that same day at their homes in Virginia and Massachusetts.

Major John Handy (1756-1828) was an Anglican patriot and merchant whose family moved from Somerset County, Maryland to Newport and owned an extensive farm south of the Old Stone Mill. Their farm was later subdivided into lots and streets named after the Handy sons Levin, William, Thomas and John. The street named after Levin was widened in 1970 and renamed Memorial Boulevard West.

THE BOSTON TEA PARTY

Captain Peleg Clarke (1734–1803) of Newport spent the better part of 1773 on the ship *Fletcher* sailing from Newport to Africa, then to Jamaica, then to London. It was the final leg of his triangular voyage back to New England and the vessel was loaded with molasses, hemp, canvas and a few crates of tea. Clarke innocently sailed into Boston Harbor on 27 November 1773 during the riots that preceded the Boston Tea Party.

He wrote London agent John Fletcher vividly describing the sacking of East India Company agent Richard Clarke's house and recounting the promise of additional bloodshed if his cargos of tea were allowed to land. Peleg Clarke managed to unload his own tea, at a loss, and sailed to Newport on 16 December 1773.

Captain Clarke's
letter dated
28 November 1773.

Mr Fletcher   Boston 2d Novmr 1773
    Sir,
                                                              the Town of
Boston is in as great an uprorore as they were at the Stamp
Act about the Tea that is acomuing here to Mr Clarke & the
other Agents, that night Mr Clarke arrived his Brothers
& sisters all came to his Fathers to make merry on the ocation
& about 8 oclock in the evening the Mob surrounded his
Fathers House & strove to break open the Doors & somebody
Fired a Pistole out of the window which so Inraged the
People that they Broke all the windows & every thing
Else that would give way, for it seemes the people are determ
that the Tea shall not Landed and it is generally thought
that if they attemt to land it there will be blood shed on the
occation, & Likewise hear that Tomorow there will be a Town
Meeting called by the Desire of Mr Clarke as they have
something to propose but what the event will be I cannot
tell as the people are much Inraged and it is not only
Thought but said that if they do not give up about the tea
that they will loose their lives Capt Hall arrived this day
with part of the so much Detested tea wich has set the
whole Town in a foment & where it will end I am our
I cannot tell but as Cato says tomorow is the great and
Important Day big with fate,

        I am Sir with Compliments to self Doctr Ewins
    & Family Your obt Humble Servt.
To John Fletcher Esqr   Peleg Clarke

THE NEWPORT POST OFFICE

Long before Priority Mail shipping, Newport's Post Office was a place of priority to Newporters in the know.

The modern Post Office system was an innovation of Benjamin Franklin who established himself as Postmaster General of the American colonies while in Philadelphia. In 1745 he appointed Thomas Vernon the Deputy Postmaster of Newport, a position Vernon held until the Revolution began in 1775.

Thomas Vernon (1718–1784) was the Tory brother of local merchants and patriots Samuel and William Vernon, of the Vernon House and the United States Navy Board. He was later imprisoned for his loyalist activities; the NHS holds the journal he kept during his captivity.

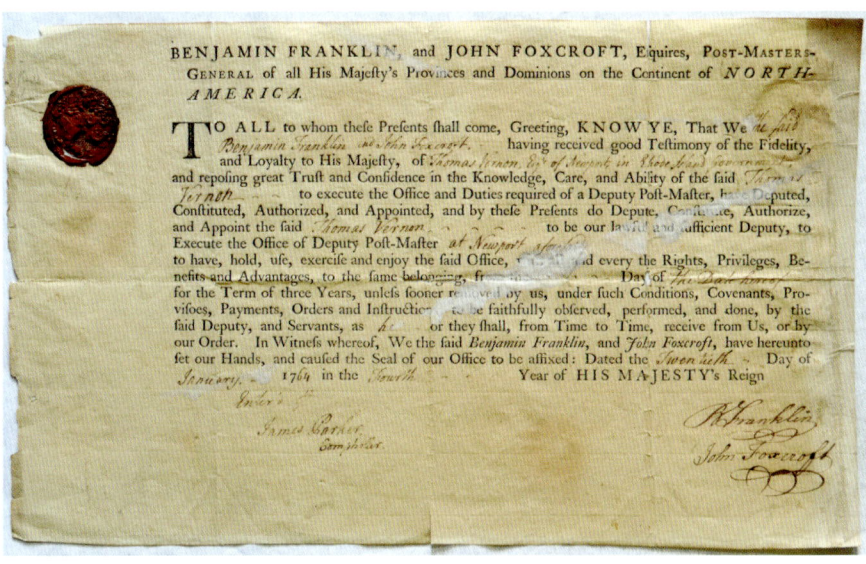

Signed by Benjamin Franklin and bearing his heraldic seal, the document pictured here appointed Vernon Deputy Postmaster of Newport on 20 January 1764 for a three year term. The Newport Post Office was located several doors south of the Brick Market on Thames Street.

Three orphaned gravestones that rest outside NHS headquarters.

ORPHANED GRAVESTONES

Many Newport gravestones have been lost to development, theft and vandalism. Stones have been found as far away as Long Island used as shoreline erosion control, patio steps and cesspool covers. Other stones were rescued from destruction by citizens including these three Newport gravestones on the grounds of NHS headquarters on Touro Street:

The 1727 GOVERNORS JOHN AND SAMUEL CRANSTON tablet stone rests in two sections. The broken stone was replaced in 2003 with a full size reproduction cut at the John Stevens Shop on Thames Street, where the original was also made.

The 1808 ELDER WILLIAM BLISS gravestone was rescued from Bliss graveyard at Green End Avenue in Middletown. William Bliss was the pastor of the Seventh Day Baptist Meeting House.

The 1739 SAMUEL AND WAITE CARR tablet stone, marketing the graves of a father and daughter who died of the small pox epidemic on the same day, was rescued during the Goat Island Torpedo Station development.

SLAVERY AND LOTTERIES

During the colonial and early federal eras, lotteries were held to raise money for public and private projects such as building a school or church, laying a road or opening a mine. Anyone with cash could purchase tickets. Apprentices, servants and enslaved individuals bought chances for the same reasons people play the lottery today.

Newport Gardener was a slave in 18th century Newport. While the information currently available is contradictory about whether Gardner bought or was granted his freedom, it seems clear that he, and three associates, won the proceeds of a lottery in 1791. The award is mentioned in several letters and reminiscences from the early 19th century with the following confirming newspaper report:

> *Salem Gazette* 10 May 1791
> No. 17221, which drew 2000 dollars in the Semi-annual State lottery, was paid on Friday laſt, by Meſſrs. Leach and Foſdick, in Boſton. The proprietors were four Africans belonging to Newport.

Gardner actively earned money while he was enslaved by hiring himself out whenever he had any free time. This practice was common in urban New England. If he bought his freedom, and that of his family, it was not because of a single stroke of luck, but rather from years of hard work.

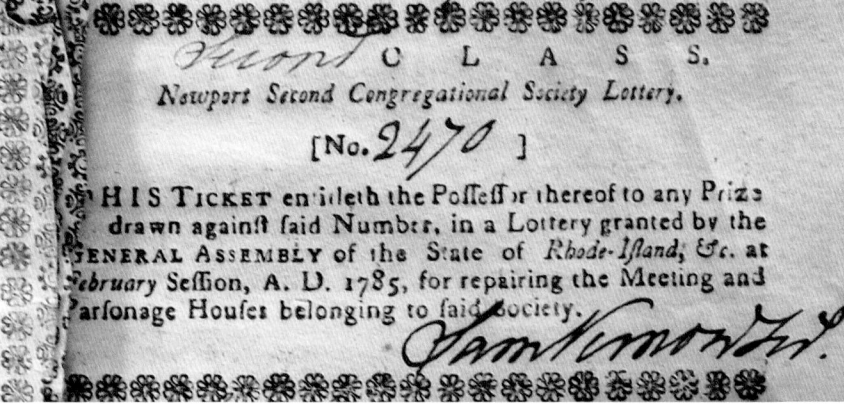

A 1785 lottery ticket signed by Samuel Vernon III, probably printed on the Franklin Press. Tickets were issued by the Second Congregational Church on Clarke Street to raise funds toward the restoration of the church and parsonage which "were in a great measure destroyed" by their use as a British army hospital during the occupation.

MEMORABLE RHODE ISLAND NAMES

Over thirteen generations and five centuries, countless people have been born and named in the Ocean State. The following are examples of unique Newport names and naming patterns from the past:

ROYAL PAINE   Several generations of Royal Paines can be found among the descendants of Anthony Paine, an original 1638 settler of Portsmouth.

PRESERVED FISH   The grandson of the early Portsmouth settler Thomas Fish. He is one of many generations including a whaler, China Trade merchant and a founder of the New York Stock Exchange, Kinsman to statesman Hamilton Fish and Newport hostess Mrs. Stuyvesant Fish of Crossways.

GRIZZEL FISH   The brother of Preserved Fish.

ISRAEL FISH LAKE (1792–1870)   Mr. Lake was a prominent merchant and shopkeeper of "Lake's Corner" at Equality Park.

DODGE – BALL   A gravestone on Block Island shows the intermarriage of founding families Tristram Dodge and Edward Ball.

CHARITY BALL   The daughter of Edward Ball.

MAHERSHALLALHASHBAZ DYER (d. 1670)   Mr. Dyer was the son of Quaker martyr Mary Dyer.

Signatures of two memorable names, Royal Paine as listed in the John Banister Account Book (1746-1749) and clippings found in Preserved Fish's c.1795 account book.

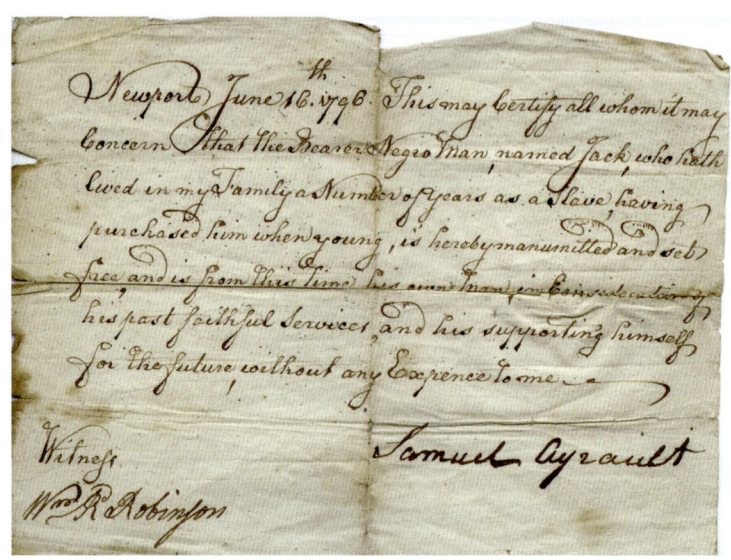

Manumission certificate executed by Stephen Ayrault for the Negro Man named Jack dated 16 June 1796.

MANUMISSION DOCUMENTS

After the American Revolution, slave ownership in Newport declined rapidly. This was largely due to moral and religious movements fueled by local clergymen and the Society of Friends. In addition, the ruined economy made slave ownership an expensive and unnecessary practice.

Many enslaved African Americans were granted freedom in wills and manumission papers, often taking new names to reflect their free status, such as Freedom, Freeset and Liberty. Some former slave owners contracted with their former slaves for paid work or helped them enter into apprenticeship agreements.

19TH CENTURY NEWPORT

USS CONSTITUTION

In the summer of 2012, "Old Ironsides" sailed around Boston Harbor for the first time in 15 years to celebrate the 200th anniversary of her War of 1812 victory over a British frigate.

The country's oldest commissioned war vessel, the *USS Constitution* was launched in 1797 and visited Newport in August 1798 with great celebration and fanfare. She returned to Newport several times and served as the official training vessel of the U.S. Naval Academy while it was located in Newport during the Civil War.

Sister ship *USS Constellation* had a longer presence in Newport as a training vessel associated with the Naval War College at Coaster Harbor Island. The Newport Historical Society has many documents outlining the *Constitution's* various repair and outfitting orders during the early 19th century.

A 1906 photo of the U.S.S. Constitution.

Detail of the envelope from the 1814 letter Capt. Taylor wrote to Mrs. Taylor.

THE NATIONAL ANTHEM'S NEWPORT CONNECTION

The bombardment of Fort McHenry in Baltimore inspired *The Star Spangled Banner* by Francis Scott Key. Newport heroes Oliver Hazard Perry and his captain William Vigneron Taylor had just completed their triumphant return after the Battle of Lake Erie, when in July 1814 they were ordered to Baltimore to oversee the construction and outfitting of the 44 gun frigate *Java*.

The British blockade delayed completion of the vessel and Perry commanded a small land battery of sailors during the September attack. Meanwhile, Captain Taylor had witnessed the torching of Washington, D.C. and sent a vivid description to his wife in a letter from Baltimore dated 30 August 1814, which is now part of the Historical Society's document collection.

1898 American flag that is believed to have been used in the Spanish American War.

History 28 Bytes

JANE STUART

One of the memorable characters from 19th century Newport was Jane Stuart (1812–1888), portraitist and youngest daughter of the artist Gilbert Stuart. Living in Boston with limited means, Jane supported herself by completing her father's unfinished portraits while studying art under instructors such as her brother Charles.

She moved to Newport in 1862 and permanently settled at 86 Mill Street. Financially strapped, she struggled to maintain her household among the trappings of Newport's Gilded Age by painting copies of her father's works. All the while, she was brilliant, witty and playful, and had a passion for charades and dressing in costumes.

Jane Stuart dressed as Cinderella's proud sister.

Three sepia photographs of Jane Stuart from Mrs. Griswold's Charades, 13 September 1866.

Jane Stuart portraying a gorilla.

Jane Stuart outfitted as "Mrs. Briggs."

THE *CHARLES W. MORGAN*

The prize of Connecticut's Mystic Seaport is the world's oldest whaling ship, the 1841 *Charles W. Morgan*. Yet few know of the origins of her name and her Newport connections.

Charles Walin Morgan (1796–1861) was a Philadelphia-born Quaker who married Sarah Rodman of New Bedford in 1819. He was in the spermaceti oil and candle business founded by his wife's connection to the Rodman and Rotch families from Nantucket and New Bedford. In 1841, Morgan built the ship bearing his name, but shortly after the whaling industry started to decline. He then invested in Pennsylvania iron and steel works.

The ship was passed down to kinsman Col. Edward Green, the son of financier Hetty Green "The Witch of Wall Street," who died childless in 1935. His heirs donated the decayed vessel to Mystic Seaport in 1941.

A photo identified as the *Charles W. Morgan*.

SANTA CLAUS AND NEWPORT

The Quakers and former Puritans of colonial Newport did little to celebrate the Christmas season. Quiet reflection, a special sermon delivered from a pulpit and the hanging of decorative greens, were the extent of 18th century festivities at Trinity Church. The Victorian era brought the decorations, music and "merry" celebrations that define the modern Christmas season.

Our modern Santa Claus has close Newport ties. Clement Clarke Moore (1779–1863), a classics scholar and Episcopal vestryman, summered on Catherine Street. He was widely known for authoring the 1823 poem *A Visit From St. Nicholas*, commonly known today as *'Twas The Night Before Christmas*. Though he wrote this story to entertain children, it has inspired much of what is considered traditional at Christmastime including the modern vision of Santa Claus.

Inspired by Moore's poem and its descriptions of St. Nick, political cartoonist and satirist Thomas Nast (1840–1902) refined the modern image of St. Nicholas as the large, bearded, jolly elf in the 1881 edition of *Harper's Weekly*. Nast himself was best known for his stinging images of Boss Tweed and the Tamany Hall gang of New York and creating the political icons of the donkey and elephant. While visiting Newport, he made a drawing of himself being posted for late payment at a local drinking establishment.

Clement Clarke Moore's desk, made by Duncan Phyfe in New York, is on display at the Museum of Newport History.

Clement C. Moore's Newport home *The Cedars*.

A 19th century Valentine from the NHS collection.

VALENTINES

Embossed paper lace Valentine greeting cards first appeared in England around 1803 and, thanks to advances in printing and manufacturing, they increased in popularity. By the 1840s, giving Valentine cards was a widespread practice in America.

The daughter of a Plymouth sea captain and bookbinder, Esther Allen Howland (1828–1904), of Worcester, MA, was at the forefront of Valentine card manufacturing. She started producing cards in 1847, shortly after her graduation from Mount Holyoke College. Esther's business flourished through the 1880s, when she sold her interest to the George C. Whitney Company who continued to produce her card designs until 1941.

Esther was a direct descendant of John Howland of the Mayflower and shared family ties with many Newporters including Catherine Howland, the wife of architect Richard Morris Hunt.

"Stadt Huys," at Coenties Slip

Illustration from Mary L. Booth's *History of the City of New York,* 1867.

MRS. GEORGE T. DOWNING

George T. Downing (1819–1903) was a prominent African American caterer, hotel owner and entrepreneur as well as a civic leader who moved to Newport from New York about 1845. His wife, Serena Leonora deGrasse, had a family lineage dating back to the earliest years of New Amsterdam. Her father, George deGrasse, was born in Calcutta and was the adopted son of the family of Admiral Count deGrasse of American Revolution fame and a close acquaintance of Aaron and Theodosia Burr in New York. Serena's mother was Maria Van Salee, sixth in descent from Abram Jansen "The Mulatto" Van Salee, Moroccan born resident of Brooklyn in 1658. After Van Salee's death, Director General Peter Stuyvesant placed his children under the care of the Orphan Master and the Dutch Church and their descendants mixed freely with the Anglo-Dutch of New York for generations.

TWELVE YEARS A SLAVE

The Oscar winning motion picture *Twelve Years a Slave,* based upon the memoir published in 1853, tells the story of historical figure Solomon Northup and his life in Louisiana as a free man of color kidnapped and sold into slavery.

Solomon's origins can be traced directly back to the Northup family of North Kingstown, who arrived from Providence before 1671. Solomon's father Mintus belonged to the John Holmes Northup family that migrated from North Kingstown to Hebron, NY around 1788. John's sons Nicholas Northup and Henry Bliss Northup of Sandy Hill, NY both offered testimony used to grant Solomon his freedom in 1853. The Northups descended from the Bliss and Carr families of Newport.

Name							
Mitchell, Ephraim	1	....	1	....	....	....	2
Mitchell, Ephraim Jr.	1	1	1	2	....	....	5
Mitchell, Thomas	1	1	1	1	....	....	4
Mowry, John Mercht.	1	3	2	2	....	....	8
Mowry, Benjamin	1	1	1	2	....	....	5
Miller, Thomas	1	1	2	2	....	....	9
Macomber, Jeremiah	1	1	1	2	....	....	5
Mowry, John	1	5	2	....	....	....	8
Northup, Immanuel	1	....	1	....	....	7	9
Northup, Robart	3	3	3	1	....	....	10
Northup, Gideon	3	4	2	2	....	....	11
Northup, John	1	2	1	2	....	3	9
Northup, William	1	6	1	....	....	....	8
Northup, Joseph	4	....	2	1	....	1	8
Northup, Rufus	3	....	2	....	....	....	5
Nason, James	1	2	1	....	....	....	4
Northup, Stephen	2	1	2	....	....	2	7
Northup, Francis	....	2	3	3	....	....	8
Nichols, George	3	....	2	....	....	....	5
Nichols, Thomas	2	2	1	1	....	....	6
Northup, Lebuas	1	3	1	2	....	....	7
Northup, Carr	1	4	1	....	....	....	6
Northup, Rowse	1	4	1	2	....	....	8
Nichols, Benjamin	1	3	1	3	....	....	8

Detail from the 1774 census data that lists the Northups.

THE FINAL RESTING PLACES OF OLIVER HAZARD PERRY

Commodore Oliver Hazard Perry (1785–1819) spent his adult life at sea, except for a brief time at his Touro Street residence with his young family. He died of yellow fever at Port-of-Spain, Trinidad on 23 August 1819, on his 34th birthday, and was promptly buried at Lapeyrouse Cemetery after an elaborate funeral at Holy Trinity Cathedral.

Following an Act of Congress, Perry's remains were exhumed and sailed to Newport on 27 November 1826 aboard the *USS Lexington*. On 4 December, a large funeral procession began at Clarke's Wharf carrying Perry's remains to the Common Burying Ground where he was interred next to his father. The procession included a carriage fashioned after the *USS Lawrence*, his Lake Erie flagship, followed by a crowd of dignitaries.

In 1843, Perry was moved again to his final resting place at Island Cemetery next to the granite and marble obelisk that the State of Rhode Island finally completed after a 16-year delay.

Details from the December 1826 issue of *The Newport Mercury* outlining Oliver Hazard Perry's funeral procession.

FUNERAL PROCESSION.

1. Three Marshals abreast, on horseback.
2. Independent Military Companies.
3. United States Troops.
4. United States Marines.
5. Rev. Clergy of different denominations.
6. The Officiating Clergyman.
7. Eight U. S. Seamen as under Bearers, and one bearing a broad pendant.
8. *Navy Captain.*   *Navy Captain.*
   Navy Captain.   CORPSE.   *Navy Captain.*
   Navy Captain.   *Navy Captain.*
9. RELATIONS of the Deceased.
10. Committee of Arrangements, supported by Marshals.
11. U. S. Seaman, bearing an Ensign, supported by two others.
12. Officers of the United States Navy.
13. Thirty-two U. S. Seamen, four abreast.
14. Officers of the United States Army.
15. Militia Officers of this State and Vicinity, in uniform.
16. Sheriffs of the State, and Deputies.
17. Banner of Rhode-Island, borne by a Revolutionary Soldier.
18. Governor and Lt. Governor of the State, supported by Aids.
19. Members of the Senate of this State.
20. Other General-Officers of the State.
21. Members of the House of Representatives.
22. Society of Cincinnati.

THE FINAL RESTING PLACES OF COMMODORE MATTHEW C. PERRY

Commodore Matthew C. Perry, brother of Commodore Oliver Hazard Perry, War of 1812 hero, also had internment issues following his 1858 death. As a resident of New York City, Perry's remains were buried in his wife's Slidell family vault at St. Mark's In-The-Bouwerie Church in lower Manhattan.

In 1866, at the request of his daughter Caroline and her husband August Belmont, Perry's remains were moved to his native Newport and buried at Island Cemetery in what is now known as Belmont Circle. For almost one hundred years, biographers and New Yorkers were reluctant to let go of Perry, claiming his remains were still at St. Mark's.

In 1953 the mayors of Newport and New York had to prove Perry's whereabouts by producing the transfer certificate from the Department of Health as well as opening the Slidell family vault to prove that Commodore Perry was no longer present.

A mounted photograph depicting the Commodore Matthew C. Perry Monument in Touro Park, which was built in 1868.

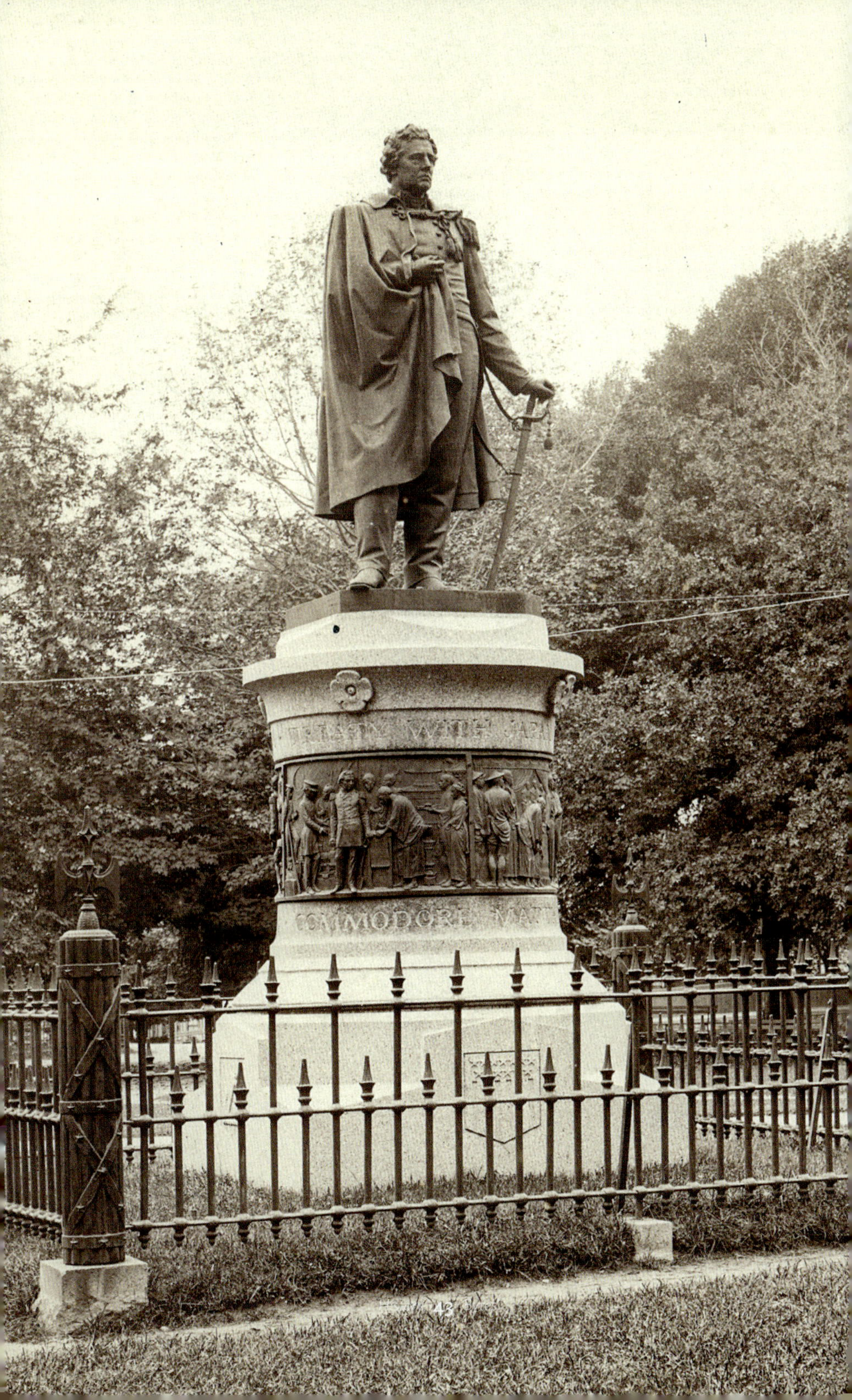
COMMODORE

A c. 1895 photo of John Austen Stevens.

FRAUNCES TAVERN

John Austin Stevens (1827–1910) of Rhode Island Avenue was a prominent historian, author and editor. He served as librarian of the New-York Historical Society and secretary of the New York Chamber of Commerce.

In 1875 he founded The Society of the Sons of the Revolution, a hereditary organization for descendants of Revolutionary Officers, who could not qualify for membership in the older and more exclusive Society of the Cincinnati. In 1904 Stevens and the Sons of the Revolution purchased Fraunces Tavern in lower Manhattan and established a museum which celebrates George Washington's 1783 farewell banquet for his officers, his final act as Commander-in-Chief of the Continental Army.

Stevens spent his final days in Newport and his papers are part of the Historical Society's extensive archives and manuscripts collection.

EDWIN BOOTH OF MIDDLETOWN

In the late 19th century, the Indian Avenue section of Middletown was marketed to wealthy New York and Philadelphia families by the Sturtevant family for summer cottage sites. One investor was the actor Edwin Booth (1833–1893), who was introduced to the area by the Bispham family of Philadelphia, who were friends and partners in the development.

Edwin Booth, brother of John Wilkes Booth, the assassin of President Lincoln, purchased lots in 1879, and in 1883 he commenced building "Boothden," his summer cottage. "Boothden" was originally designed by noted architect Calvert Vaux, whose son Downing Vaux was engaged to Booth's daughter Edwina. The scandalous break-up of Downing and Edwina hampered the building process, and Booth waited out the summer in hotels and guest houses as builder Truman Peckham completed the house in 1884.

Edwin Booth spent four years at "Boothden." Money problems, Edwina's subsequent bad marriage and his brother's legacy took a toll. The house, which would not sell, was willed to Edwina in 1893, and ultimately sold in 1903.

A note of historical irony: located one half mile away off Vaucluse Avenue are buried the remains of Baptist minister Obadiah Holmes (1606–1682), Abraham Lincoln's fourth great grandfather.

A photo of Edwin Booth before 1893.

EDWIN BOOTH.
EAST GRAND CIRCUS PARK, Detroit.

NEWPORT AND PRESIDENT LINCOLN

In April 1865, John Wilkes Booth was a guest at the Aquidneck House Hotel in Newport shortly before the assassination of Lincoln in Washington, D.C. The hotel was located on the west side of Corne Street, between Mill and Pelham Streets. The site is now occupied by modern, colonial-style condominium townhouses.

The Historical Society holds several items associated with President Lincoln including military commissions and a silver tassel from his catafalque.

Silver wire and wood tassel from the drapery of the catafalque upon which the remains of President Lincoln were carried from Washington, D.C. to Springfield, Illinois in April 1865.

History **49** Bytes

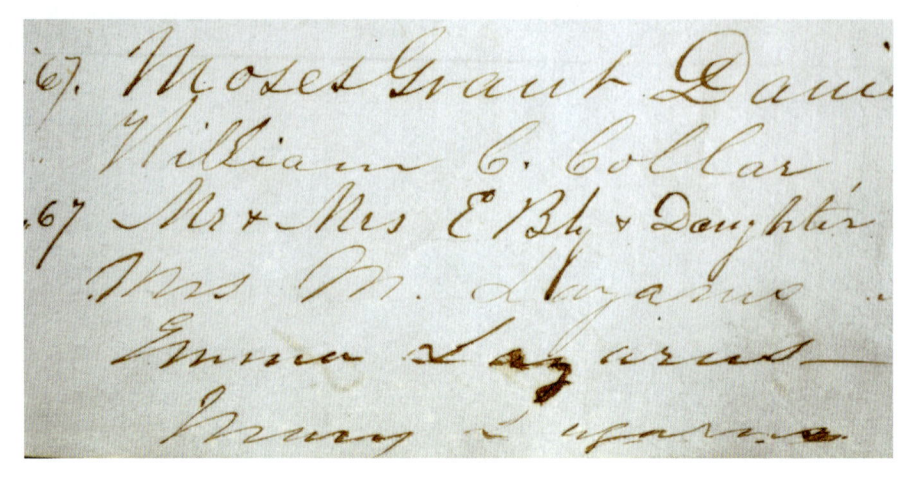

Emma Lazarus's name as it appears in the Touro Synagogue Visitor Book, courtesy Touro Synagogue.

EMMA LAZARUS

"Give me your tired, your poor, your huddled masses yearning to breathe free…"

These familiar lines from the sonnet *The New Colossus* were penned by Emma Lazarus (1849–1887) in honor of The Statue of Liberty. Poet, essayist and champion of Jewish refugees, Lazarus spent summers with her family at "The Beeches" on the corner of Bellevue Avenue and Lakeview Avenue, next to "Belcourt Castle." Her first appearance in Newport was on 25 July 1867 when she, at age 18, and her father Moses Lazarus, signed the Touro Synagogue Visitor Book.

A c. 1914 glass plate negative depicting the Moses Lazarus Estate, also known as "The Beeches" and "Wyndhurst," located at the corner of Lakeview and Bellevue Avenues.

ANNA HARRIETTE LEONOWENS

Shall we dance?

After lovingly caring for the 82 children of King Somdetch Phra Paramendr Maha Mongkut, King of Siam, Anna Harriette Leonowens (1831–1915) toured America to promote her memoir *The English Governess of the Siamese Court* (1870).

Anna lectured at the Newport Opera House on 8 February 1872 and participated in Julia Ward Howe's Town & Country Club, where writers, feminists and abolitionists mingled. Anna's memoir was the basis of the popular Rodgers & Hammerstein musical *The King and I*.

The NHS archives and manuscripts collection holds documents with the signatures of two Siamese kings, including Mongkut.

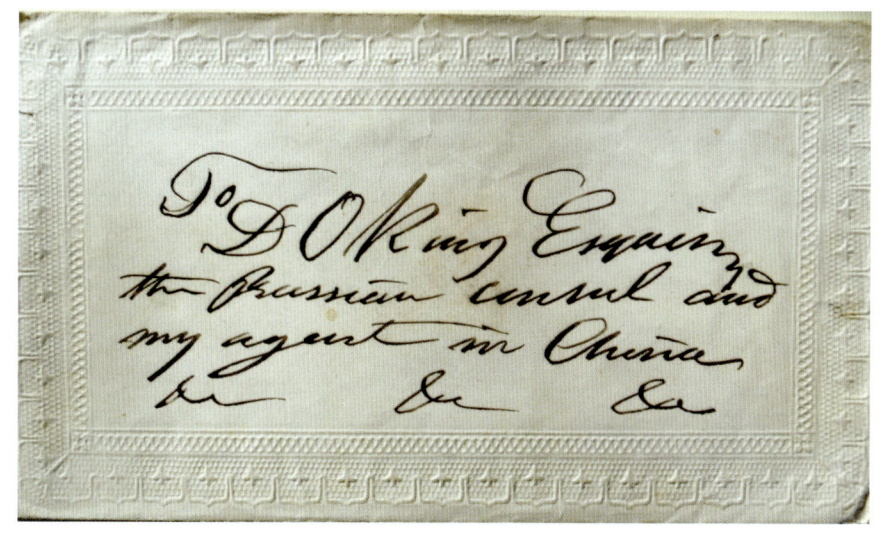

An envelope and letter addressed to David Olyphant King from King Mongkut of Siam, c. 1850.

ROLLER SKATING IN NEWPORT

The Atlantic House Hotel on Bellevue Avenue and Pelham Street, having been abandoned by the U.S. Naval Academy in 1865, was seeking new guests and activities for the summer. In July 1866 the hotel contracted with James. L. Plimpton of New York to provide rooms for the New York Skating Association to introduce the new pastime of roller skating to Newport.

Stereograph depicting the Newport Skating Rink on Bellevue Avenue by Newport photographer Joshua Appleby Williams before 1892.

Known as "rinking," roller skating developed in the parlors of European aristocracy and was imported to America by Plimpton in 1863. In 1879 the Ocean House Hotel constructed a new rink, now the site of the Newport Casino grandstand. It hosted roller skating polo and "circling" around the rink, which was enjoyed by "educated and refined patrons" and later opened to the general public.

CALLING CARDS

During the Gilded Age, dropping by a friend's house was acceptable and encouraged as long as such visits conformed to an extensive menu of rules and regulations. Calling cards were an essential element in this exercise with an additional set of requirements outlined in over twenty pages of Ward McAllister's book *Society As I Have Found It* (1890).

In short, upon arrival at the house, the card was presented to the head butler at the front door, forwarded to the lady of the house who would decide whether or not to receive the visitor. Specific corners of the card would be folded down to indicate the lady's wishes or her absence.

Three calling cards from the NHS collection.

Mr. Ward McAllister.

16, WEST 36TH STREET.

Mrs. Stuyvesant Fish.

109 East 30th Street.

Mr. & Mrs. Astor.

A c. 1906 photograph of greenhouses at "Rockhurst" on Ledge Road. From the Henry O. Havemeyer Collection, Newport Historical Society.

NEWPORT GREENHOUSES

Gardening, often considered the most popular American hobby, is more frequently classified as the number one summer chore. During the Gilded Age, many summer cottages had their own greenhouses, also called hothouses, located on site. Managed by a professional master gardener and a large staff, these structures sometimes exceeded the footprint of the family home which they served. They provided the flowers for arrangements throughout the house as well as shrubs and trees for the loggias, terraces and grounds.

"BEECHWOOD"
John Jacob Astor
340,437

A detail from an 1893 atlas marking the location of several greenhouses.

190,000
"MARBLE HOUSE"
Alva E. Vanderbilt

William Waldorf Astor
366,878   "BEAULIEU"

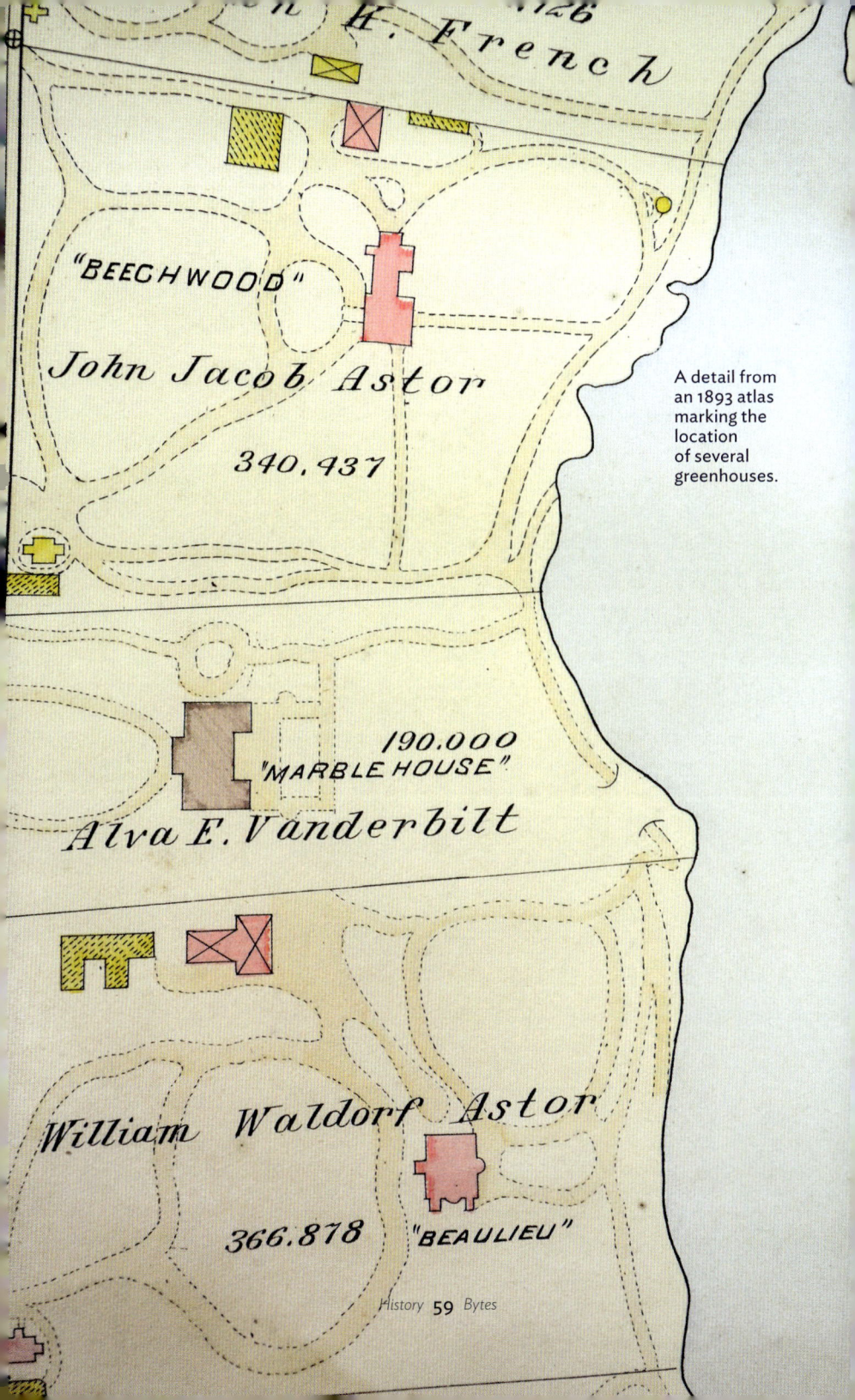

History 59 Bytes

POINSETTIAS AND NEWPORT

The delicate Mexican plant that adorns houses during the Christmas season was developed by Joel Roberts Poinsett (1779–1851), diplomat, politician and Member of Congress.

Poinsett, of Charleston, SC, spent most of his career shuttling between Washington and South America, Cuba and Mexico. He later served as Secretary of War.

In 1833 Poinsett married Mary Izard Pringle, a member of the extended Henry Middleton family of Charleston and Newport, and visited with family living on Washington Square, Bellevue Avenue and Pell Street. Great grandson Joel Roberts Poinsett Pringle studied in Newport under Admiral Sims and later served as President of the Naval War College 1927–1930.

Joel Roberts Poinsett c. 1844. Image courtesy the Library of Congress.

JOHN SINGER SARGENT IN NEWPORT

In October 1887 the *Newport Journal and Weekly News* reported, "Mr. J. S. Sargent of London, who has become somewhat renowned as a portrait and figure painter, is in town and is staying with Mr. H. G. Marquand on Rhode Island Avenue."

John Singer Sargent (1856–1925) was born in Florence to a prominent Philadelphia family, with many ties to the American families of the Gilded Age, and his Newport subjects included the Marquands, the Cushings and the Boits. In Newport he stayed at "Linden Gate," the Henry G. Marquand cottage on the corner of Rhode Island Avenue and Old Beach Road. Marquand was a financier, philanthropist and Board President of the Metropolitan Museum of Art in New York. "Linden Gate" passed to son-in-law Roderick Terry, a president of the Newport Historical Society, and was destroyed by fire in 1973.

A 20th century photograph of Marquand House, also known as "Linden Gate" located on Rhode Island Avenue.

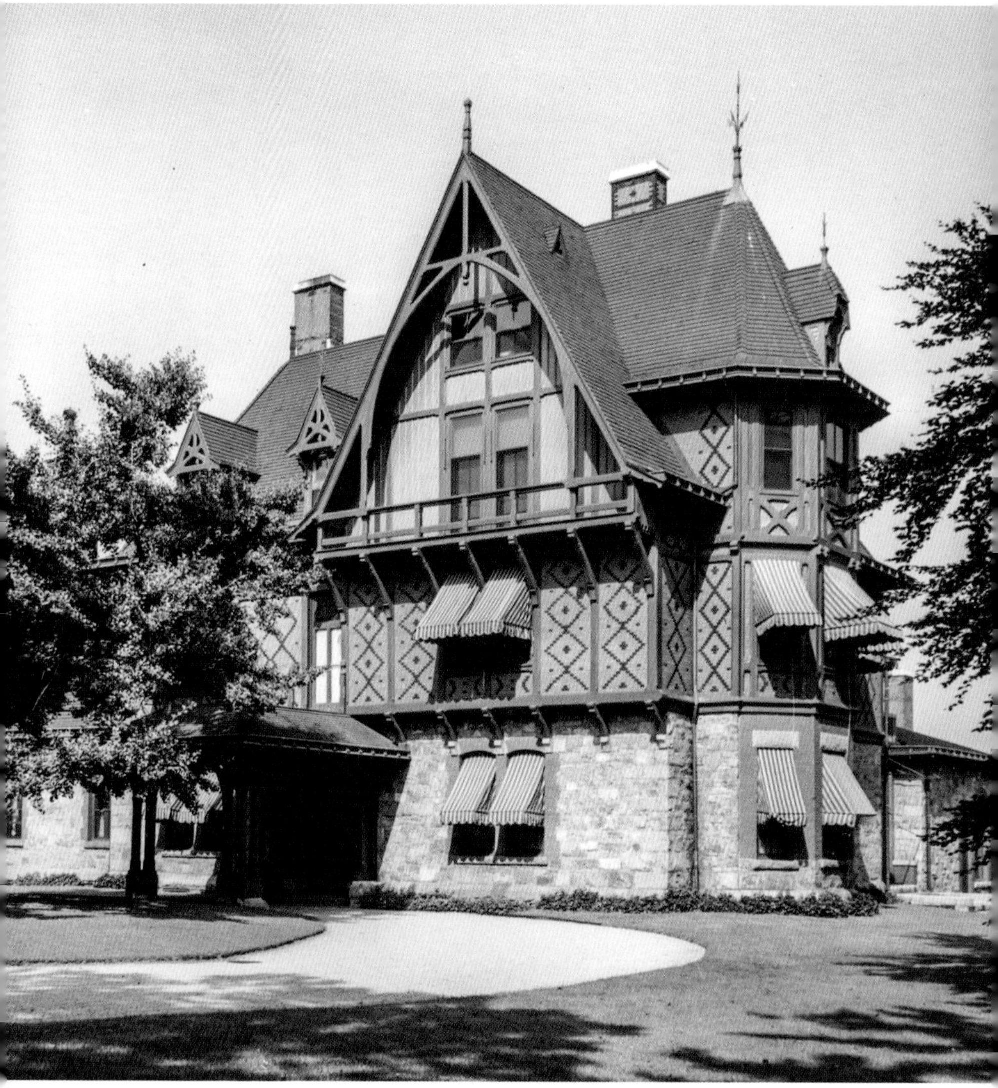

An 1864 photograph of "Beaulieu" located on Bellevue Avenue.

NEWPORT'S ROYAL WEDDING

During the season of 1899, the William Waldorf Astor family summered in Europe and rented their Bellevue Avenue cottage "Beaulieu" to Chicago socialite and philanthropist Mrs. Potter Palmer. On September 23rd, Mrs. Palmer hosted the wedding of her niece Julia Grant to Major General Prince Michael Cantacuzène of Russia. The Russian Orthodox ceremony was performed in a specially built chapel next to the main salon. The American ceremony took place at All Saint's Episcopal Chapel on Old Beach Road ten days later.

Julia Grant was born in the White House in 1876 when her grandfather Ulysses S. Grant was President. Prince Michael was commander-in-chief of the Russian army under Grand Duke Nicholas and later led the last great cavalry charge of 15,000 Cossacks against the Austrians after having been shot. Michael and Julia fled to Sweden during the revolution; they eventually settled in Sarasota, Florida and were subsequently divorced.

20TH CENTURY NEWPORT

NEWPORT'S *TITANIC* PASSENGERS 1912

Several passengers on the ill-fated luxury liner *Titanic* were Newport residents or visitors. They include:

John Jacob Astor of "Beechwood," located on Bellevue Avenue, perished. Mrs. Astor, who was six months pregnant, survived and gave birth to J.J. Astor V who lived until 1992.

"The Unsinkable Molly Brown," Margaret Tobin Brown of Colorado, rented the Meunchinger-King cottage on Redwood Street and Bellevue Avenue. She was the suffrage partner of Alva Vanderbilt at a Marble House rally.

William Earnest Carter and his family all survived. They lived at "Quarterfoil" on Narragansett Avenue.

William C. Dulles, who lived next to Carter family, perished.

Margaret B. Hayes survived and married Dr. Charles Easton. She is buried at St. Mary's Episcopal Church in Portsmouth, RI.

James Clinch Smith and family, who lived at the corner of Harrison and Halidon Avenues, perished.

George D. Widener of Philadelphia perished. His wife, Eleanor Elkins Widener, survived and built "Miramar" on Bellevue Avenue in 1914. She remarried Dr. Alexander Hamilton Rice.

Karl Howel Behr and Richard Norris Williams, tennis champions who visited Newport, died.

Clarence Bloomfield Moore, visitor and Horse Show participant, also died.

The front and back of a 1912 postcard labeled "Beechwood, Residence of John Jacob Astor."

Beechwood, Newport, R. I.
Residence of John Jacob Astor.

Dear Mrs C.
My F. is much better
today D. is having
a fine time I hope
she is not bothing
you too much will
look for her Saturday
many thanks
best love to you both
snowing here today

Mrs W. Christie
14 High Street
Worcester
Mass.

May 1912
Mrs Christie

THE MALBONES OF *DOWNTON ABBEY*

The popular *Masterpiece Classic* television show *Downton Abbey* follows Lord Grantham and often highlights his financial problems. Viewers know that he, as a young owner of his estate, required an infusion of American money in order to keep it—a topic familiar to Newport heiresses.

Oddly enough, the subject of inheritance is not limited to the sets and sound stages in the hills of Berkshire. The genuine owner of the estate where *Downton Abbey* is filmed, Highclere Castle, George Reginald Oliver Molyneux (b. 1956) is the eighth Earl of Carnarvon and descends from the Stanhope family, Earls of Chesterfield.

On 14 August 1783 Sir Henry Edwyn Stanhope, captain of *HM Frigate Mercury,* married Miss Margaret Malbone at Trinity Church in Newport. He was stationed at Newport and became friendly with the Francis Malbone family, loyalists who lived on Thames Street. Sir Henry later became a Vice Admiral of the Royal Navy, Baronet and a predecessor of the Earls of Chesterfield. After the American Revolution, the couple retired to Stanwell House in Middlesex.

The c. 1758 Frances Malbone House, located at 392 Thames Street.

History **69** Bytes

"Oakwood" home of James Stillman, from George Champlin Mason's *Newport and Its Cottages* (1875) part of the NHS collection.

THE ROCKEFELLERS

John D. Rockefeller was one of the few great New York industrialists who did not have a presence in Newport; he preferred the hills of upstate New York.

His son John D. Jr. married Abigail Aldrich of Providence, RI while his brother William established connections to Newport through business partner, friend and in-law James Stillman.

The interior at "Oakwood" by Ludovici's Photographic and Crayon Studios of New York and Newport.

Descended from early Seventh Day Baptist settlers of Westerly, RI James Stillman (1850–1918) was a partner in Standard Oil, president of the National City Bank of New York and had interests in railroads with J.P. Morgan and E.H. Harriman. In 1892 he purchased "Oakwood," the old Charles Russell cottage on Narragansett Avenue and spent summers there with his two daughters who married William Rockefeller's two sons. The house remained in the family until 1922 and was later demolished to make way for "Bois Dore" in 1926.

A c. 1930 photograph depicting the airship *USS Los Angeles* (ZR-3) moored to a navy vessel, most likely off Newport.

AIRSHIPS IN NEWPORT

MetLife and Goodyear blimps have been hovering over Newport sporting events and concerts for years. The use of manned rigid airships dates to Naval experiments conducted in places such as Narragansett Bay.

In 1923 the airship *Shenandoah* (ZR-1) successfully moored on a tower erected on top of the *USS Patoka* at Newport, enabling airships to dock on vessels at sea. The airship *Los Angeles* was also moored in the bay in 1930. These local airships, which measured 680 feet in length, did not last long because of weather and exploding hydrogen.

In July 1910, Stuart Davis of Providence and John Jacob Astor of Newport devised a plan to establish airship ferry service from Hazard's Beach to Scarborough Beach at Narragansett Pier. That same month *The New York Times* reported that Wilbur Wright would deliver aeroplanes to select wealthy cottagers in August. One airship was brought up by Astor and the other was furnished by the Zodiac Dirigible Company of France. Support buildings were to be constructed at both sites.

The first flight in late August failed to reach the necessary altitude and the project was immediately scrapped.

LET'S SPLIT: THE LEVI GALE HOUSE

In 1925 officials decided to build a new Newport County Court House on Washington Square next to the historic Colony House. There was one problem: a building stood in the proposed location.

On 8 December 1925, the Levi Gale House was cut in two and dragged from the top of Washington Square to its current location at the corner of Division and Touro Streets, and then pieced back together.

Originally designed by Russell Warren for New Orleans merchant Levi H. Gale in 1835, today it houses the offices of Touro Synagogue.

The Levi Gale House in 1925, split into two parts just prior to its move from Washington Square to Touro Street.

The Levi Gale House during its December 1925 reconstruction after it was moved to Touro Street.

VAN JOHNSON

Broadway stage and motion picture star Van Johnson was born in Newport on 25 August 1916 and lived at 16 Ayrault Street. He attended Rogers High School, took dancing lessons at the Gladding School of Dance and worked odd jobs in Newport before establishing his career in New York.

The Rogers High School graduating class of 1934. Van Johnson is believed to be standing in the top row, seventh student from the left. Photo taken on Broadway on the school's front steps by Samuel Kerschner.

When Gene Kelley left the cast of *Pal Joey*, Johnson moved up from the chorus to the lead role. He went on to star in *Thirty Seconds Over Tokyo* and many other MGM hits, often returning to Newport to visit his father and attend school reunions. Johnson died in Nyack, NY in 2008 and his belongings were sold at a New Jersey auction house.

In 2010, he would have been 94; his birthday was celebrated with a party at the Jane Pickens Theater.

> Young, Mr. and Mrs. Robert R.; (Anita Ten Eyck O'Keefe)
> "Fairholme", Ruggles Avenue   Phone 4121
> Winter: Palm Beach, Florida

KING EDWARD AND KING GEORGE

The Academy Award winning movie *The King's Speech* sparked renewed interest in King George VI. The sudden abdication of the throne by his older brother King Edward VIII in 1936 propelled King George reluctantly into the forefront of pre-war Europe. After the abdication and his subsequent marriage to Wallace Warfield, the new Duke and Duchess of Windsor became regular, sought-after fixtures of American Café Society.

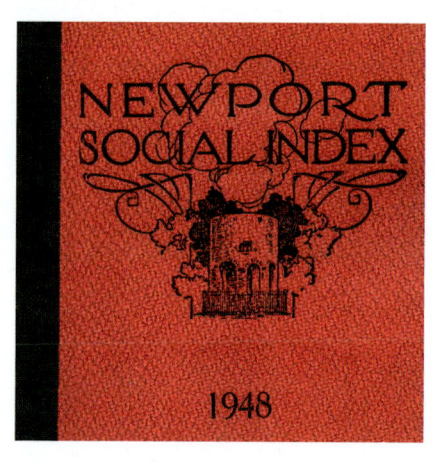

The Youngs listed in the 1948 Newport Social Index.

They were frequent guests of Robert and Anita Young at "Fairholme" on Ruggles Avenue and at other Newport homes. The Youngs owned "Fairholme" from 1942 until Anita's death in 1985. Her sister was the artist Georgia O'Keeffe.

PEARL HARBOR AND NEWPORT

The attack on Pearl Harbor immediately effected Newport's vast Naval presence. Long-time Naval War College professor Admiral William Satterlee Pye (1880–1957) was immediately placed in command of the U.S. Pacific Fleet after the swift dismissal of Admiral Kimmel following the Japanese bombing. Pye was succeeded by Admiral Nimitz, and then returned to Newport to serve as President of the War College until 1946.

Sudden changes also occurred at the U.S. Naval Torpedo Station complex on Goat Island, Rose Island and Gould Island. Women civilian workers were aggressively recruited and hours of operation increased to 24/7. By 1944 the Torpedo Station employed a total of 14,122 workers and produced one-third of all torpedoes used in World War II.

Women working at the U.S. Naval Torpedo Station on Goat Island.

THE UNITED NATIONS AND NEWPORT

In 1945 cities from around the world were invited to promote themselves as the ideal location of the new United Nations Headquarters.

Under the leadership of John Nicholas Brown and kinsman Hon. Major Sherman Stonor of Oxfordshire, Newport submitted a proposal with the support of Governor Pastore and Theodore Francis Green. Newport's ideal climate, sophisticated culture and legacy of democracy would make a perfect location, with a new headquarters building erected at Fort Adams. "Ochre Court," "Seaview Terrace" and "The Breakers" would serve as offices and embassies, and a plethora of underutilized and abandoned mansions throughout Newport would be available for purchase.

The international search committee rejected all proposals and chose donated Rockefeller land in New York City for the headquarters, started in 1948.

An Invitation to the United Nations Organization to Establish Permanent Headquarters in Historic Newport, Rhode Island
on the Island of Aquidneck --- *"Isle of Peace"*

The title page in *An Invitation to the United Nations Organization to Establish Permanent Headquarters in Historic Newport, Rhode Island.*

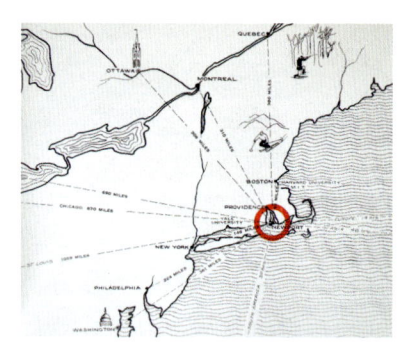

A map from the c. 1945 promotional booklet *An Invitation to the United Nations Organization to Establish Permanent Headquarters in Historic Newport, Rhode Island.*

History **80** Bytes

STATE OF RHODE ISLAND & PROVIDENCE PLANTATIONS
EXECUTIVE CHAMBER
PROVIDENCE

November 26, 1945

Mr. Gladwyn Jebb
Executive Secretary
Preparatory Commission of the United Nations
Church House, Dean's Yard
Westminster, S. W. 1
London, England

My dear Mr. Jebb:

    Confirming my cablegram, of November 23rd, I reiterate my endorsement of the invitation extended by the City of Newport asking the United Nations Organization to locate its capital in Newport, Rhode Island.

    This city is ideally located; its climate is the finest to be found on our Atlantic coast and it, I am sure, has the required facilities.

    As Governor of Rhode Island I am intensely interested in having our City of Newport selected by your organization, and assure you that I shall co-operate in every way possible in the event that our invitation is acted upon favorably by you.

Respectfully yours,

John O. Pastore
Governor

JOP:MC

A letter from the Rhode Island governor promoting Newport as a location for the United Nations.

THE KENNEDY WEDDING

On 12 September 1953, Senator John F. Kennedy married Jacqueline Bouvier at St. Mary's Catholic Church on Spring Street. A reception followed at Hammersmith Farm, the summer home of Jackie's mother and stepfather.

The wedding was covered by fashion and celebrity photographer Antionette "Toni" Frissell (1907-1988), whose family summered at "Vedimar" on Harrison Avenue and who are interred in the churchyard at St. Columba's Chapel in Middletown, RI.

The Kennedys returned to Hammersmith Farm for the last time in 1963 on their 10th wedding anniversary.

Senator John F. Kennedy and Jacqueline Bouvier Kennedy on the lawn at. Hammersmith Farm, on their wedding day. Image courtesy Toni Frissell, John F. Kennedy Presidential Library and Museum, Boston.

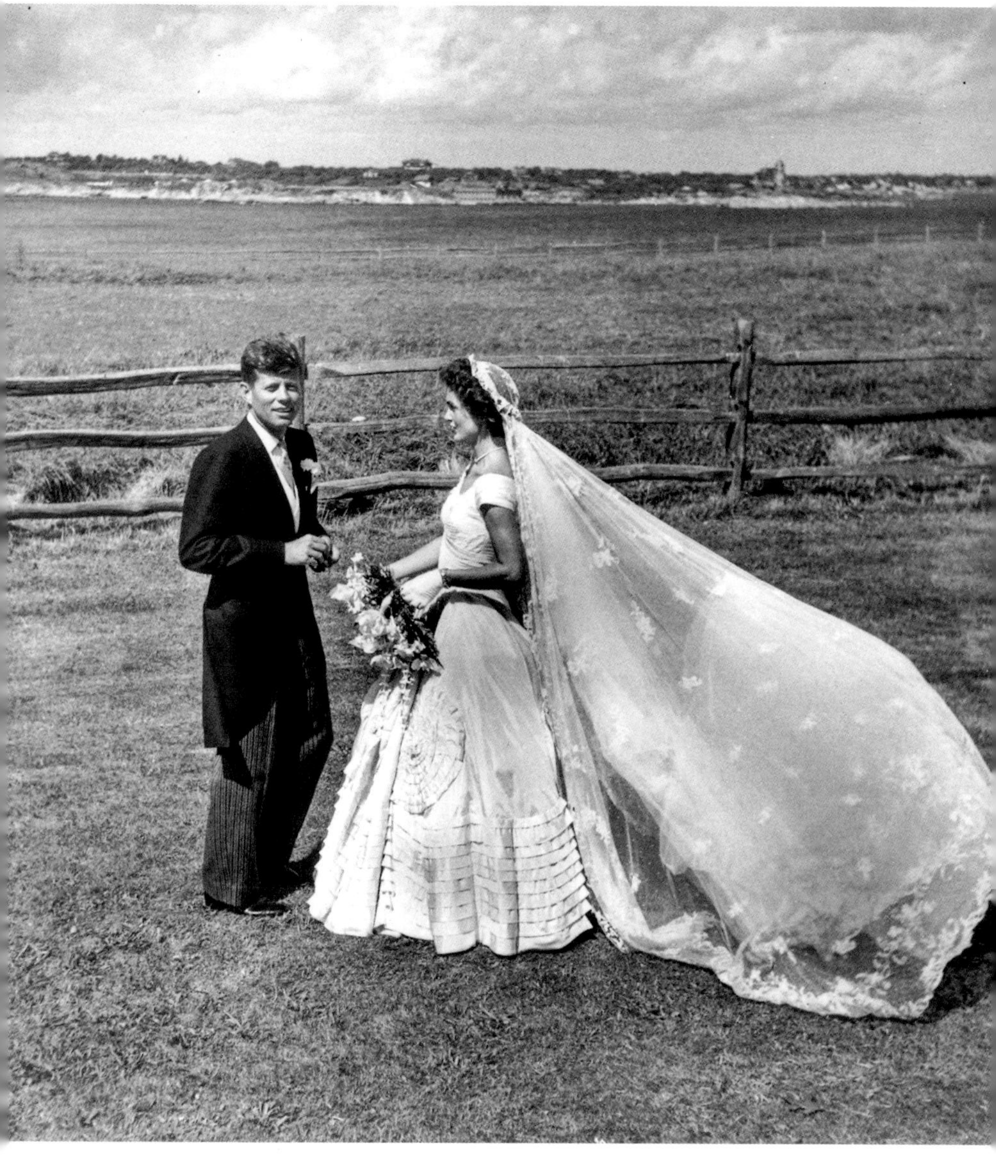

Mr. and Mrs. Hugh Dudley Auchincloss

request the honour of your presence

at the marriage of Mrs. Auchincloss' daughter

Jacqueline Lee Bouvier

to

The Honorable John Fitzgerald Kennedy

United States Senate

on Saturday, the twelfth of September

at eleven o'clock

Saint Mary's Church

Spring Street

Newport, Rhode Island

RECEPTION

FOLLOWING THE CEREMONY

HAMMERSMITH FARM

NEWPORT, RHODE ISLAND

THE FAVOUR OF A REPLY IS REQUESTED

The Kennedy's wedding invitation.

PRESIDENTIAL VISITS

Newport has long been a destination for American presidents. The following list are those presidents whose visits have been documented by the press or historians. Many past and possibly some future presidents have been house guests and dinner guests in private homes without public knowledge.

George Washington
Thomas Jefferson
James Monroe
John Quincy Adams
Andrew Jackson
Martin Van Buren
John Tyler
James Polk
Millard Fillmore
James Buchanan
Ulysses Grant
Rutherford Hayes
Chester Arthur
Grover Cleveland

Benjamin Harrison
Theodore Roosevelt
William Howard Taft
Franklin Roosevelt
Dwight Eisenhower
John Kennedy
Richard Nixon
Gerald Ford
Ronald Reagan
George H. W. Bush
William Clinton
George W. Bush
Barack Obama

There are many items in the NHS collections with presidential connections. One example is this photograph which shows former President Theodore Roosevelt (Colonel Theodore Roosevelt) meeting with Captain Edward H. Campbell, Commandant, which took place at the Naval Training Station in Newport on 17 October 1918.

History 87 Bytes

DARK SHADOWS

Gothic soap opera fans might recognize establishing shots from the popular 1970s television show *Dark Shadows* as having a Newport connection. Though the series was filmed on a sound stage in New York City, images of the cottage known as "Seaview Terrace" on Ruggles Avenue were used in the opening and closing credits. A later "reincarnation" of *Dark Shadows* featured actress Joanna Going, whose family owned the Isaac Bell House on Bellevue Avenue.

"Seaview Terrace" was remodeled by Edson Bradley in 1925 to accommodate the finished rooms he imported from his Washington D.C. residence. The mansion has served as a summer cottage and as a variety of schools.

"Seaview Terrace" on Ruggles Avenue, 1943.

History **89** Bytes

Christo and Jeanne-Claude in action. Image courtesy Salve Regina University Special Collections, William A. and Gael Crimmins Papers and Photos on *Monumenta.*

CHRISTO AND JEANNE-CLAUDE WRAP NEWPORT

In 2005, the artists Christo (b. 1935) and Jeanne-Claude (1935–2009) constructed 7,503 fabric panels on the snow covered grounds of Central Park in New York. Known as *The Gates,* it was an immediate sensation and the latest example of environmental art in their portfolio of "wrappings."

As part of the 1974 exhibit of modern sculpture in Newport known as *Monumenta,* Christo and Jeanne-Claude wrapped King's Beach on Ocean Drive. It consisted of 150,000 square feet of white polypropylene fabric attached to the shoreline. Known as *Oceanfront Project,* it lasted for eight days.

Aerial shot of *Monumenta*. Image courtesy Salve Regina University Special Collections, William A. and Gael Crimmins Papers and Photos on *Monumenta*.

CUNARD LINE VISITS NEWPORT

Massive cruise ships commonly stop in Newport Harbor each fall. The first appearance of an ocean liner was Cunard's *Queen Elizabeth 2* in 1982. Christened in 1969, the QE2 served in the Falklands War in 1982 and made several visits to Newport in the twilight of her 39 year career. In 1992 the QE2 ran aground off Cuttyhunk Island, near Buzzards Bay, suffering extensive damage to the hull. All of the passengers were safely transported to Newport.

The *Queen Mary 2* was launched in 2004 and arrived at Newport that year on Independence Day during the Tall Ships celebration. At 1,132 feet, she is the largest ocean liner built to date and makes periodic appearances in Newport.

An October 1982 *Newport Daily News* photograph showing the *Queen Elizabeth 2* visiting Newport.

AMISTAD

In 1997 Stephen Spielberg transformed the center of Newport into an 1840 Connecticut seaport to film the motion picture *Amistad*. A dirt road surface was laid on Washington Square and a prison was built in front of Trinity Church, among other temporary changes.

While Newport had no role in the famous slave uprising and subsequent trials, the Spanish schooner *Amistad* of New London subsequently ended up under the ownership of a Newport sea captain.

Preparing for the 1997 filming of *Amistad* at Queen Anne Square.

In 1841, the *Amistad* was nationalized by Congress, renamed *Ion,* and sold by the U.S. Court to Capt. George Howland of Newport. Later that year, Howland sold the schooner to the Guadeloupe Consul at Port Petre in the West Indies. Capt. George Howland (1797–1878) and his wife Sarah Almy lived in the Barney House on the corner of Touro and Spring Streets, now part of the Touro Synagogue campus.

QUEEN ELIZABETH

In June 2012 England observed a Diamond Jubliee celebration for the first time since 1897. Queen Elizabeth II celebrated her 60th year on the throne with parades, bonfires and boat flotilla on the River Thames.

In July 1976 Queen Elizabeth visited Newport for the Bicentennial celebration. She dined on the royal yacht HMS *Britannia* with President Ford and dedicated Queen Anne Square after attending services at Trinity Church. All of her children have since visited Newport.

In 2005 a 16th century financial account signed by Queen Elizabeth I (r. 1558-1603) was discovered in the Newport Historical Society's collections sandwiched between two copies of *The Newport Mercury* from the 1860s. Scribed on vellum and encapsulated in silk for conservation, the text document was identified by a handwriting expert and an English archivist as an appraisal of precious stones, probably from a captured Spanish vessel, and boldly signed by the Queen. More research is needed to further understand this faded and fragmented document and its unknown origins.

The 16th century financial document signed by Queen Elizabeth I.